Team Stats—Basketball Edition

HOUSTON ROCKETS

Nicki Clausen-Grace
and Jeff Grace

BLACK RABBIT BOOKS

Bolt is published by Black Rabbit Books
P.O. Box 3263, Mankato, Minnesota, 56002.
www.blackrabbitbooks.com

Jennifer Besel, editor; Michael Sellner, designer;
Omay Ayres, photo researcher

Library of Congress Cataloging-in-Publication Data
Names: Clausen-Grace, Nicki, author. | Grace, Jeff, author.
Title: Houston Rockets / by Nicki Clausen-Grace and Jeff Grace.
Description: Mankato, Minnesota : Black Rabbit Books, [2021] |
Series: Bolt. team stats-basketball edition | Includes bibliographical references and index. | Audience: Ages 8-12 |
Audience: Grades 4-6 |
Summary: "Discover the Houston Rockets' powerhouse players and biggest moments through exciting text and dynamic infographics"— Provided by publisher.
Identifiers: LCCN 2019050014 (print) | LCCN 2019050015 (ebook) |
ISBN 9781623102913 (hardcover) | ISBN 9781644663875 (paperback) |
ISBN 9781623103859 (ebook)
Subjects: LCSH: Houston Rockets (Basketball team)—Juvenile literature.
Classification: LCC GV885.52.H68 C53 2021 (print) | LCC GV885.52.H68 (ebook) | DDC 796.323/64097641411—dc23
LC record available at https://lccn.loc.gov/2019050014
LC ebook record available at https://lccn.loc.gov/2019050015

Printed in the United States. 2/20

All facts and statistics are current as of the 2018–2019 season.

Image Credits

AP Images: Al Messerschmidt Archive, 24; ASSOCIATED PRESS, 28–29; Ben Margot, 10–11; Bill Kostroun, 25; David Breslauer, 18–19; David J. Phillip, 15; F. Carter Smith, 23; Lennox Mclendon, 12; Mike Nelson, 20–21; Pat Sullivan, 15; Eric Christian Smith, 16; Rick Bowmer, 4–5; STEVE WILSON, 27; bleacherreport.com: Bleacher Report, 26–27; Dreamstime: Jerry Coli, 3; ebay.com: illini37, 6; P&R publications, 6; Getty: Dmytro Aksonov, 24–25; Norm Perdue, 8–9, 25; Newscom: George Bridges, 13; Troy Taormina/USA TODAY Sports, Cover; Shutterstock: Duda Vasilii, 28–29; EFKS, Cover, 1; GOLFX, 31; IfH, Cover; vasosh, 8–9, 14, 19, 21, 28–29, 32

CONTENTS

CHAPTER 1

On the COURT

It was Game 1 of the 1995 NBA Finals. The Houston Rockets played the Orlando Magic. The game had 1.6 seconds left. Rockets player Kenny Smith drilled a 3-pointer. The shot tied the game and forced it into overtime.

The game was still tight in overtime. With seconds left, the score was 118–118. Then Hakeem Olajuwon tipped in the ball. The Rockets won!

CHAPTER 2

History of the ROCKETS

The Rockets team is known for winning close games. But it hasn't always been a winning team. It formed in 1967 in San Diego, California. It had four rough seasons. It moved to Houston, Texas, in 1971. Since then, the team has made 32 **playoff** appearances. And it has won two NBA championships.

1967 team

A company built rockets in San Diego. That's how the team got its name. When it moved to Houston, it kept the name. NASA launches rockets in Houston. So the name still made sense.

TEAMS WORTH THE MOST MONEY

Teams make money through ticket sales and TV deals. They also sell items with the team logo on them.

$2.8 billion
$2.3 billion
$2.2 billion
$2.15 billion
$1.9 billion
$1.7 billion
Boston Celtics
Brooklyn Nets
Houston Rockets
Los Angeles Clippers
Dallas Mavericks
Miami Heat

CHAPTER 3

Greatest MOMENTS

Winning seasons are made up of many great moments. One of those moments was January 3, 2019. The Rockets played the Golden State Warriors. The Rockets came from behind and tied the game. In overtime, **defenders** were all over James Harden. With two seconds left, he nailed a 3-point shot. The Rockets won!

Rakuten
WARRIORS
30
ROKiT
HOUSTON
13

SAMPSON
50

Picking a Winner

Game 5 of the 1986 Western Conference Finals was tough. The Rockets and Los Angeles Lakers were tied. There was one second left. Ralph Sampson took a pass. He threw up a shot. The ball bounced around the rim and fell in! The Rockets went to the NBA Finals.

The team mascot is Clutch the Bear. Its name celebrates winning in a "clutch" or close game.

Champs!

It was the 1994 NBA Finals. The Rockets and New York Knicks were tied at three games each. The Rockets led 80–75. Then with less than two minutes left, Vernon Maxwell hit a 3-point shot. The Knicks didn't have time to catch up. The Rockets won its first NBA championship.

Hakeem Olajuwon was named the Finals MVP in 1994.

NBC

HOUSTON
15
MAGIC
10
adidas
MAGIC
11
HOUSTON
13
MAGIC
25
PAYTON
2

A Big Triple-Double

In 2018, James Harden had an amazing game. He scored 60 points, grabbed 10 **rebounds**, and dished out 11 **assists**. Harden made NBA history that night. He became the first player to score a triple-double with 60 points.

triple-double — scoring at least 10 points, 10 rebounds, and 10 assists in a game

Rockets Team Records

By the Numbers

65
most **wins** in a season

139–87
score of biggest **win**

80–136
score of biggest **loss**

156 most points scored in a game

14 fewest wins in a season

66 fewest points scored in a game

KIA

CHAPTER 4

ROCKETS Superstars

Rockets fans love watching their stars. One of those stars is James Harden. Harden **averages** about 29 points per game. He was the 2017–2018 season MVP. And he's gone to the All-Star Game seven times.

Harden scored at least 30 points against all 29 NBA teams. He did that in one season. That's an NBA record.

Calvin Murphy

Calvin Murphy played all of his pro **career** with the Rockets. He has the second-most career points for the team. He was a great helper too. Murphy is the team's career leader in assists.

Rockets Career Assists Leaders

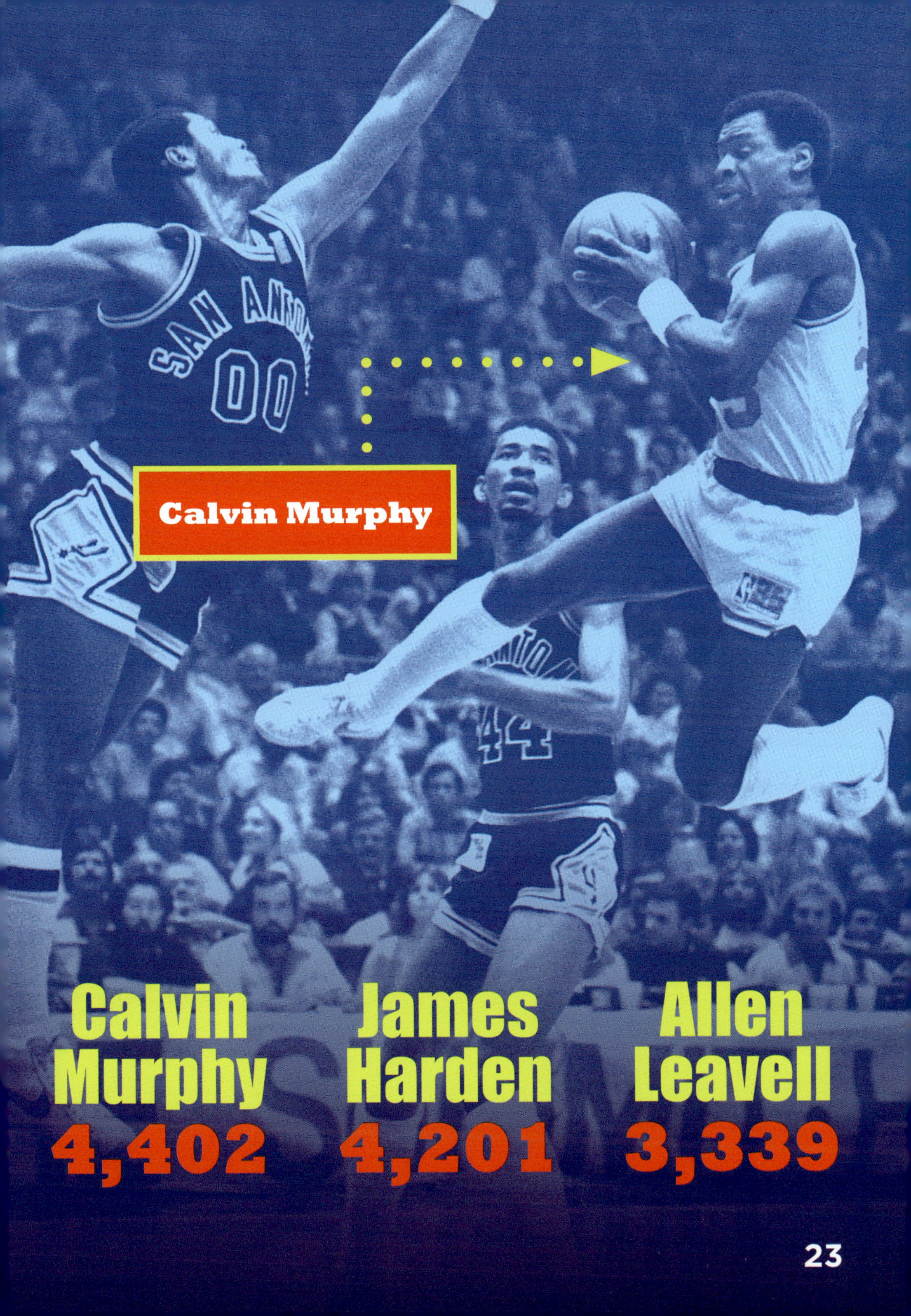

Calvin Murphy
4,402

James Harden
4,201

Allen Leavell
3,339

Hakeem Olajuwon

The Rockets got the first pick in the 1984 **draft**. They chose super-tall center Hakeem Olajuwon. He would go on to lead the Rockets to two NBA titles.

The Dream Shake

Olajuwon had a move called the "Dream Shake." The move faked out defenders so he could score.

Olajuwon has the ball near the basket.

Step 1

Olajuwon was great on both ends of the court. People call him an all-time great center. He was voted one of the NBA's 50 greatest players.

Rudy Tomjanovich

Rudy Tomjanovich helped the Rockets on and off the court. He played 11 seasons with the team. Then from 1991 to 2003, he was the team's head coach. He coached it to both of its championship wins.

The team seems to play best when things get tough. Fans can't wait to see what it does next.

ROCKETS TIMELINE

1967

The team forms.

1984

The team drafts Olajuwon.

Team wins second NBA championship.

2018

1994

1995

Harden scores 60-point triple-double.

Team wins first NBA championship.

GLOSSARY

assist (uh-SIST)—the action, such as a pass, of a player who helps a teammate to score

average (AHV-rij)—a number that is calculated by adding quantities together and then dividing the total by the number of quantities

career (kuh-REER)—a period of time spent in a job

defender (de-FEN-dur)—a player who works to stop the other team from scoring

draft (DRAFT)—a system in which new players are chosen for professional teams

logo (LO-go)—a symbol used to identify a company

playoff (PLAY-ahf)—a series of games played after the regular season to decide which player or team is the champion

rebound (RE-bownd)—to take possession of the ball after it bounces off the backboard or rim

BOOKS

Flynn, Brendan. *Houston Rockets All-Time Greats.* NBA All-Time Greats. Mankato, MN: Press Room Editions, 2020.

Kelley, K. C. *Houston Rockets.* Insider's Guide to Pro Basketball. Mankato, MN: Child's World, 2019.

Whiting, Jim. *Houston Rockets.* The NBA: A History of Hoops. Mankato, MN: Creative Education, 2018.

WEBSITES

Basketball
www.ducksters.com/sports/basketball.php

Houston Rockets
www.britannica.com/topic/Houston-Rockets

Houston Rockets
www.nba.com/rockets/

INDEX